SWEATSHIRT

Jordan Stewart

GALLEON

Sweatshirt

First Galleon Edition, December 2025
ISBN 978-1-998122-29-5

Published by Galleon Books
Moncton, New Brunswick, Canada
www.galleonbooks.ca

Sweatshirt and its artwork were conceived, written, edited and designed in New Brunswick, Canada

Cover & Inside illustrations by Pamela Marie Pierce
Author photo by Amy Stewart

Library and Archives Canada Cataloguing in Publication

Title: Sweatshirt / Jordan Stewart.
Names: Stewart, Jordan, 1983- author.
Identifiers: Canadiana 20250326183 | ISBN 9781998122295 (softcover)
Subjects: LCGFT: Poetry.
Classification: LCC PS8637.T49456 S94 2025 | DDC C811/.6—dc23

For my girls:

The Blonde
The Chaos
The Noodle

Tired Eyes

Other Worlds Than These

Love, or Something Like it

ONE / **Tired Eyes**

Let's Get Started

Let's start with some honesty:

Will we ever see a log truck on the highway
and not consider death?

Can we admit the slightest excitement
when opening *all* mail?
Us, taking turns being *occupant*.

Watches are just an attempt
to get a handle on dying.
Aren't all rooms waiting rooms?

The joy of camping is in the starting over.

The top of the fridge will never be clean.

Dog tongues are like a weird slug.

Other people's kids are worse than your kids.

Love is a fever dream.

Coffee is an alcoholic's run at noon.

Eating peanut butter out of the jar for lunch
four times a week doesn't represent
healthy, or intelligent life choices.

Ok.

That's enough honesty for now.

The Valedictorian and a Massive Hangover

On days like this, even the grass is a sleepy shade of grey,
as if whoever colored the sidewalks went way outside the lines.

The kids are cutting school, and the teachers don't care;
they sit in their classrooms with the valedictorian, and a massive
hangover.

It's cold but could be colder, and we're old but getting older.
The housewives are taking migraine pills with their morning coffees.

The neighbors are moving slowly to fix their fences, or walk their dogs.
The day's air is filled with homemade tattoos and car trouble.

It's the kind of day to write a novel set in an elevator
or call your father to appreciate station wagons with faux-wood
panelling.

These are days imagined by colorblind cab drivers
who've invented cars fueled by awkward silences and talk of the
weather.

Today everyone's a runner on third with two outs –
a little lonely, a little nervous, but with something to look forward to.

In the Garage

When it warms, we live in the garage,
a half-hearted attempt at being outside.
Listening to the rain, but never feeling it.

We roll the doors up and watch the night
happening out there without us.

A racoon comes in and asks us what time it is,
and why our legs can hold up our entire bodies.
We feed him peanuts and call him Bandit.

We build a treehouse in the yard but never sit in it.
We mow the lawn, but never picnic on it.
We hear the summer happening just outside.

The late July heat feels like swallowing cotton.
Only the dull, grey cement floor
knows the secret to staying cool.

"Do you think stars only exist
as a projection of our insecurities in the modern world?"
Bandit is asking us, shelling a peanut.

We watch the leaves outside gush, gasp, redden, and fall,
blowing in panicked circles
that trend slowly toward our open doors.

When the snow finally does come,
we abandon ship, driving the cars in,
reserving our winter ideas, for the inside warmth.

Bandit is saying goodbye,
"I'll miss you, but also
I'd be a terrible house guest."

Expiration Dates

I'm sitting quietly on my brand-new couch,
struggling with the imposition of expiration dates.

The milk promises it will be here for another two weeks,
but the rubbing alcohol in the bathroom wants commitment.

Wants to be here until May, five years from now
and I am trying to find a way to let him down gently.

It's not that I don't value the friendship; it's just...
I'm not sure how I feel about the possibility
of being outlived by rubbing alcohol.

It's almost as if a year doesn't exist
until you see it referenced for the first time

in a furniture commercial. They're promising that, yes,
you can take this leather recliner home, today,

and not pay a dime until two thousand *thirty*.
I'm always a little uncomfortable by the honesty of this new
number.

"It's just... let's not get ahead of ourselves, you know?"
I'm saying to the rubbing alcohol.

I'm talking with my hands a lot,
like I sometimes do when I'm nervous.

A Reckless Precedent (Five Dollars)

I've had a five-dollar bill
in my pocket for about 2 months.

It's folded and tangles occasionally
with Costco receipts and a toonie
I found on the entry table.

The toonie is fated for a school lunch
or the Terry Fox walk.

Toonies for Terry, they'll say.

As if alliteration
is the key to my generosity.

The fiver remains though,
a temporary bookmark
in a slow-moving book of poetry.

A teeth cleaner,
or a place to jot a phone number.

A visual reference for
a complicated story
concerning a rectangular building.

The bill will find its eventual home
as a tooth fairy's offering.

"Five dollars!?" My wife will say later,
"A dangerous, and reckless precedent
has been set this day."

Cat, Previously

Rain, like a phone message
pulsing, endlessly.

A female voice fills the house,
pours in and around the corners

filling the darkest parts.
Under the bed, behind the couch,

it's not a voice I recognize,
not one I've spent time with.

I try and picture, in my mind,
what this voice's lips look like,

working together with tongue and teeth,
pushing words through my phone and under my bed.

"This is All Creatures Vet," she is saying.
"Carl Winslow is due for his checkup."

I look over at the cat who's perched
on the back of the couch.

He stares back at me, knowingly,
twitching an ear in faux nonchalance.

We're quiet for a while, Carl and I,
the plastic phone, and the rain.

Cat, Currently

He's in the garage
staring at the
open floor drain
after a mouse
who's disappeared
into the night.
Disappeared
through the pipework
into the
drainage ditch
in the backyard,
where the summer's leaves
go to die by the
wheelbarrow load.
The cat
who doesn't understand
drains,
or wheelbarrows,
or disappearing mice,
or red lasers,
or calculating
compound interest.
The mouse
Shawshanks
out the drainpipe
in the backyard
and into
the cool night-air.
Tiny whiskers
rub against
dead leaves
and the noise
travels back up the piping
to a floor drain,
and to a cat that

doesn't understand much –
but knows escape
when he hears it.

A Note from You

You're getting on OK,
but your landlord is a difficult person
to get a hold of (to arm wrestle with?).

The grocery store near you is large
but doesn't have grapes worth a damn,
or the toothpaste you like.

It doesn't have those faux-Italian pizzas either,
as if faux-Italians are not native
to that particular region.

Work's been going ok.
Your alarm clock's broken and your boss
doesn't like when you come in late,

He doesn't like your work reports either –
you file them wrong – and the two of you can't agree
on how to spell neighborhood.

The police are good to you though,
and the drunk tank is roomy,
the kind of place a man can be proud to wake up in.

The kind of place you can talk to Albert,
the cop on duty, about his disrespectful kids,
and failing marriage.

I finger the lined paper, picturing the two of you
on either side of the metal bars,
wondering which one I should feel sorry for.

Night Artist

I'm sitting on the third-floor balcony
of a complete stranger's uptown apartment.

The night is cool, but I can't see my breath,
so I'm smoking cigarettes instead.

In the distance I can see a man spray painting a giant cock
on the side of a rusted train car.

He stops occasionally,
and the rattling of his can carries in the autumning air.

Just down the street from the train yard
I can see the empty tennis courts.

The lights are still on, but the players have long gone home,
the empty green courts yawning like open bear traps.

The spray painter finishes, and stands back, admiring his work.
He's got some real talent, I think, and I wish I could tell him so.

I hear movement from the apartment behind me,
so I climb the rail,

descending the latticework
to the street below.

No Guts, No

She smokes cigarettes
but calls them fags.
"Everybody's doing it," she says,
and I look around,
to make sure I'm not a supporting actor
in a public service announcement.

The smoke's a cruel mistress,
and my lungs reject it immediately –
my lungs,
having higher standards than I –
my lungs,
who aren't trying to impress anyone.
I inhale again, and they settle.

"Settle down, you inside bags,"
I say to my lungs.
"You're just guts,
you're not the boss of me."

I inhale again,
and they protest again.
"No guts, no," I'm saying,
my voice,
strained with smoke.

Poetic Obligations

Well,
fuck poetry then.

Handsome little line-breaks
and words,
words.

On days it wants to talk to me
about things like
love, or birds,

I won't be listening.

I will pretend to be
on a fishing trip
(Gone fishin'!)

or growing tomatoes
in the garden.
(Gone Tomatoin'!)

It will show up later though
it always does.

A sunrise,
or an empty playground,
or the ocean,
and I'll feel bad.

"Your hair is the sun
and the morning is a
brand new way for us
to be honest,"

I will say quietly,
through clenched teeth.

How I Lost the War and Bought Cable

There's been a mop on the neighbor's roof since April.
One of those standard, wooden-handle jobs
with the twisted white strings
your younger brother learned to slow dance with.

It's sitting pretty squarely in the middle,
at a bit of an angle, with the moppy-bits
all fanned out like a whole pot of spilled spaghetti
or Baby Spice doing a backflip.

I look out across the street for hours at a time,
making little notes in a ragged Campfire Notebook.
Like how, after a good rain, the area around the mop
is always the last place to dry.

Or last week when a violent windstorm
moved the stringy bits up just a bit,
and the mop sort of resembled a torch
being held by someone running very fast.

This morning, though, things changed forever.
I'm leaning back, sipping fresh coffee,
making a note about how I thought the mop
might look in the winter, under a layer of snow,

when suddenly the neighbor – shirtless, and angry –
charges around the side of their house with a ladder.
I drop my feet from the front of the fridge, sitting upright,
my chair landing with a loud thud.

"No. Fucking. Way," I say to myself.
The man's sweaty back charges up the rickety ladder
until he's standing squarely between me and the mop,
eclipsing my view for the first time in months.

Reaching down, the bare-backed son-of-a-whore
picks up the mop and throws it down into
his out-of-sight, fenced-in backyard.
A sound like choking comes from somewhere in my throat.

Then, in a final act of attrition,
he turns, looking directly at me from atop his roof,
points his middle and index fingers into his own eyes, and
then, forcefully, in my direction.

He turns his back to me once more
and ambles down the ladder, leaving me speechless,
staring at a darker, mop-shaped spot on his roof,
and quietly leaving a mop-shaped hole in my heart.

Outside In

The day we went inside,
a mother black bear died three area codes away.
She was shot trying to see
what the inside of an apple looks like,
or to be more truthful, what it tasted like,
and let's be truthful for a minute.

When we were younger
we'd stand on the wood pile behind your house,
looking in through the back window
to watch your older brother and his girlfriend
run their hands over each other.
Your older brother,
who was missing three fingers
from a chainsaw accident.

The day we went inside,
a bridge collapsed in the neighboring county,
killing some homeless people sleeping underneath,
inconveniencing half a dozen soccer moms.
The next day's headline would read:
"Bridge collapses, soccer practice canceled."

Months from now, we'll laugh together,
smoking cigarettes on the same aging wood pile.
We'll count the stars overhead,
blowing smoke at them
while we smell the neighbor's fresh cut grass.
Like a mother black bear;
sniffing apples from the outside in.

Shift Work

There used to be something romantic about 4 am;
the quiet newness, and still-shaky legs,
of a brand-new day.

The air used to be electric,
like you were doing something you shouldn't be,
as if you were part of a secret club,
and in a way, I guess we were.

In the car, during the dark winter mornings,
the heater works overtime defrosting windows.
The snow knows your car all too well,
and makes its way inside, riding pant cuffs.

An unmanned CBC plays Aboriginal talk radio,
and I turn it down but not off, to remind myself
I'm not the only person on the planet.

My small car noses itself onto
a barely cleared street,

and I follow growing snow banks and fading street-lights
all the way home.

All Applicable Sales Tax

Head down,
pulse up,
one foot
then the next –
he speed-walks
through Wal-Mart
like it owes him something.

It doesn't, of course.
In fact, on the contrary,
he owes it
the price of the blue Gatorade
bulging in his back pocket,
plus all applicable sales tax.

The floor manager,
huffing like a vice principal
gunning for that promotion,
swarms the sliding doors
and runs out
to the sidewalk,
yelling and waving
and I can't decide
who to root for.

Warm Cans of Old Milwaukee

She talks about drugs the way a rookie salesman sells a car:
honestly, and for far too long.

Mother always says that girls like her wear too much lipstick
and go through life without bank accounts.

We're sitting in the back of the all-night theatre
when she tells me to close my eyes, and then kisses me.

When the movie ends, I ask her to marry me.
She laughs, pulling me out of the theatre and into the night.

She leads me to the bridge, where we drink warm cans of Old
Milwaukee.
Mother always says that only trolls and bums hang out under bridges.

A few months later, it's Christmas time.
The snowy streets smell like dusty computer parts.

I'm window shopping with my mother
for overpriced candle holders and small porcelain cats.

She's inside telling a store owner (who used to be a pro baseball
player)
his prices are too high, and she wants a discount.

I wait outside patting a blind man's dog
while he tells me about his ex-wife and his favorite songs about rain.

Down the street I see the girl, getting in a car with an older boy:
the kind of boy that grows a moustache and high-fives too often.

I pretend not to notice, staring at my snowy boots.
Mother always says that moustaches are for cowboys and drunks.

Sea Street for a Second

The ocean has stolen the show one too many times,
and I am not prepared to grant it yet more poetic audience.

The cold November air carries my breath as I sit on my front porch,
watching my neighbor prepare her yard for winter.

I consider it a thankless task,
but she finds the joy in it anyway.

This is a day, so quiet and still,
I can't help seeing the beauty in everything.

I remember you once asked me
if being beautiful was all it was cracked up to be,
and I laughed, telling you I honestly wouldn't know.

My other neighbor, across the street,
is inside having sex with identical triplets.

He knows their names but not which is which,
and I can only suspect that while having sex with identical triplets,
sorting names may not be the priority.

I think this street is a perfect street,
and I imagine a movie director walking past.
He stops, seeing the same things I do,
and instantly decides to make a movie here.

I smile and stand, and wave him over.
I say that I've been expecting him,
and would he like some hot chocolate?

And nevermind the ocean.

Snow Day on Sea Street

The snow was falling quickly but quietly
on an unassuming Thursday morning.
It's slowly erasing the back-lawn beer cans,
and rusty, white-brown patio furniture.

Our snow pants gave our bodies a lisp
as we slid and swished down the sidewalk towards the ocean.
We stood on the edge of it, looking out over the water
as it lapped on the shore, apparently unaware of the snow day.

"Take a break!" we yelled at the ocean,
our mouths pushing cotton at the sky.
"Can't you see it's snowing?" we asked,
but the ocean keeps working, like it always does.

Later, we walked home, revisiting our old steps,
leaving fresh ones in their place.
Visions of hot chocolate and Muppet Christmas carols
danced in the back of our minds.

"I read some place," you said, "That a single snowstorm
can have the energy of one hundred and twenty atom bombs."
The falling snow made your voice sound very hollow and far away.
I thought that maybe the ocean was just lonely.

Sea Street in Late April

The sidewalks are trying to be summer again,
and we are happy to oblige their premature fantasies.
We've taken no solace in February's long attempt
at sweatering us and feeding us half-pizzas.

Suddenly we're out the door and gone,
plunging into the ocean's heartfelt breezes,
jackets and sweaters stripped off quickly
like mid-to-late winter band-aids.

My neighbor to the immediate left
is from Boston and swears a lot about things like
broken lawn chairs, the weather, Canadian beer,
the Bruins, the fog, untied shoelaces, taxes, and Tuesdays.

Even now, on newborn days like today,
with the sun treating our winter eyes unkindly,
we're struck with just how quiet this place is,
how much this place feels like it belongs to us.

A flock of geese pass overhead in one direction;
a jumbo jet cruises by in the other.
Who are we to take sides? Lying on the unmowed, damp grass
of an unsold suburban home.

TWO / **Other Worlds Than These**

Sweater Weather

The day the box shows up,
the morning air is dry and cool.

I look out the window
to see its perfect shape in the intersection:
3 feet high, 3 wide, 3 deep.

(A cube, if you will.)

Outside, standing on the sidewalk, a crowd is forming.

"I'll tell ya this, in my day, a cube was just a cube,"
an old man is saying.

Neighborhood kids are taking turns almost touching it
before the police show up with their lights on,
but sirens off, as if their cruisers
are at a loss for words.

At night, the agents erect giant lights around the cube,
while people in hazmat suits
run their rubber hands over the edges,
fingering the sharp corners, searching for an imperfection.

A dog somewhere barks rhythmic in the night

"Rawp, rawp, rawp, rawp"

The local newspaper decides to nickname the cube
Sweater Weather for the coming season,
calling it sweat-wet for short,
which I think is kind of gross.

The hazmat suits are cutting the street pavement,
making a huge square around the box.

"Looks like a big square dent
in the taxpayer wallet if you ask me,"
the old man is saying.

When they try to lift the box, the crane breaks.
Later, a helicopter trying to do the same nearly crashes.

The news vans double overnight.

When the street pavement under the box falls away,
and nothing is holding it up, they double again.

My landlord raises my rent.

"In my day, cubes obeyed the simple laws of physics,"
the old man is saying.

On December 19th, 6 days before Christmas,
the box disappears.

"Every time a weird alien box disappears,
an angel gets its wings," the old man is saying.

I stand at the window,
staring at the gigantic square hole in the street
full of nothing but pipes for water and gas
that run and split in every direction,
like twisted bones in a concrete earth.

The street is finally quiet again,
save a dog's lonely voice, barking rhythmic in the night.

"Rawp, rawp, rawp, rawp"

The Comforting Sounds of Bank Robbery

"I've got an idea," she says.

The cadence of her voice spoils her excitement
as she rolls the paper flat on the kitchen table.

"Are these... blueprints?" I ask.

"Please hold all questions for the end," she says.

Outside in the cold night,
the snow falls slowly, like it doesn't really want to,
like it has other things on its mind.

Somewhere upstairs a sleeping child
rolls over in their bed, before settling.

"As you can see there are entrances
here, here, and here."

"Is this... the bank?" I ask.

Our dog wanders in,
his toenails click rhythmic on the tile floor
like he's typing an important email.

An email about delayed food refills,
or declining tennis ball quality.

The fridge clicks on, hums.

"We can park the car here," she continues.
There are cameras here, here, and here."

"How long have you been working on this?"

She forges on, "The security guard's name is Curtis,
He's supposed to work 8-hour days but actually only
puts in like 6 and a half."

"Curtis!"

The wind picks up outside
and the house braces itself against the storm.
The aging wood flexes and creaks;
creaks in a comforting way.

An Aluminum Afternoon

Mechanical rain clouds grind by slowly
on these aluminum afternoons.
The sky is checkered with blue steel –
cold, unforgiving seams and bolts.

We're sitting on the beach
running our fingers through the coffee grinds,
watching a rusting sun move along the track,
disappearing behind the skyscraper skyline.

A ship on fire sails past us
in the brown coffee ocean,
its cannons firing children's shoes into the waves,
percolating in the fishing weirs.

In the distance, a man wearing a tuxedo
is walking down the beach toward us.
When he reaches us, he stops
and places both hands in his jacket pockets.

"Would you like a mint?" he says,
his mouth: a bowling alley on fire.
"Yes, we would like a mint," we reply,
our mouths: just, regular mouths.

The mint brings my insides to life,
skittering to and fro, across the pink of my tongue.
Cartwheels and jumping jacks
laced with drug, and fine upholstery.

The man in the tuxedo tips his hat
and turns, walking directly into the ocean.
The cool breeze stings my peppermint mouth
as I watch his hat slip beneath the waves.

Our hands touch beneath the soggy grinds,
and I feel your skin for just a second.
It's the only real thing about this place,
and I revel at the touch of it.

The shiny brass trumpets
are washing ashore by the dozen,
and the children run,
laughing and gathering them for the fire.

An hour later,
we're standing beside a fire taller than us,
watching as it curls around the brass buttons
and reaches toward the steel sky.

The children laugh and run in a circle around the flames,
carelessly weaving around us.
A young boy loses his footing in the grinds
and collapses into the blazing trumpets.

In a flash, you reach into the flame,
grab him by the shorts, and pull him out;
he looks up at you and laughs,
while the burnt skin falls off the cold steel of his face.

And when the same thing happens
to the skin on your right hand,
I look out over the brown water,
pretending not to notice.

Cause & Effect

The anchorman had forgotten his glasses
on his new girlfriend's nightstand
and kept losing his place in the teleprompter,
causing him to stutter and pause.

Which, in turn, caused the people watching at home
to bang on the sides of their televisions
in an attempt to fix the sound.

He was trying to tell them
about the impending hurricane,
to warn them to get out of their homes,
to evacuate.

They couldn't hear the thunder
for the television banging,
and when their feet started getting wet,
they yelled for someone to "jiggle the handle."

There would be no survivors.

Fuck Onions

You're in the bathroom putting black stripes under your eyes.
You're not sure why people do this,
but you're fairly certain it's a war thing, or a football one.

You come charging out and jump on the couch,
putting one foot on the arm.
You pause, pointing at me, screaming "HEART FIGHT, BITCH".

I immediately rip open my shirt, then my chest.
Blood runs down my forearms, dripping off the back of my elbows.
(You always hate when I claim that elbows have a back.)

You do the same while moving the coffee table.
You rear back, holding your beating heart behind you like a scorpion tail.
I take a more neutral stance, gripping it like a baseball at my side.

We circle each other, slowly, staring each other down;
a fine red stream courses from our hands and chests.
"Not this time. You're going down."

"I hope you got your plot picked out cause I'm gonna BURY YOU."
"I hope you kept your receipt cause I'm gonna render you DEFECTIVE."
"I hope you're not asleep on the train cause this is the END OF THE LINE."

The ensuing battle resembles something between mud wrestling
and the last scene of a Jean-Claude Van Damme movie.
It would be three hours before we collapsed, exhausted.

"Pizza?" you ask, slipping your heart back inside your blouse.
 "Yeah, sure," I reply, my chest heaving as I catch my breath.
"But no onions, dude; fuck onions."

Déja Vu Train

An overnight train ride filled with
retired bankers and bank robbers.
There's an air of familiarity between them all,
but no one can quite pin it down.

This déjà vu train car winds its way
between the green mountain trees,
and my newspaper dutifully reports:
train accidents on the rise.

The train attendant is making her way down the aisle.
She stops at my seat and asks me if everything is ok,
and I tell her it is.
She has a face that you immediately
want to be very close to, for a very long time.
I don't mean that she's a kitten,
but I don't mean she isn't one either.

I imagine that there is a very grand mystery
unfolding a car or two back.
I'm an extra in the twisting roller coaster
of an Agatha Christie novel.

A mysterious murder
and a torn piece of a checkered overcoat
snagged on the splintering wood of an aging seat.
Everyone's a suspect.

The rain beats down on the side of the train,
and I stare out into the black.
The loneliness is thick on a ride like this,
and you can almost touch it.

I look around at the oriental carpeting
that lines the entire floor of the car.

As if everybody's waiting for a drummer to set up,
but none ever does.

The bankers and the robbers have agreed to sleep on it for now,
and I decide to join them.

Home School

She places a small red apple
on the wooden dresser to her immediate left.

She says that, for the rest of the day,
that apple will be called a toothpick.

Later that day, in the garden,
we're burying the second mailman of the week.

She tells me that mailmen are sent to us occasionally
to help us fertilize the soil and grow healthier flowers;

that we must use every part of the mailman,
and she hands me another pair of blue cargo shorts.

Inside, after supper, we're sitting at the table
eating freshly baked toothpick pie.

She tells me I will start school tomorrow
and that the classroom will be in the den.

My teacher will look and sound exactly like her
but will not actually be her.

I lay awake that night, staring at the ceiling,
thinking about what school will be like,

wondering what things I will learn
and if the teacher will like my cargo shorts.

Bandits Came in the Night

The town folk are gathering in the square.
They've called a meeting to discuss a recent windfall.

Better books for the schools, or better roads
or exactly how many hardware stores a town actually needs.

The men have working hands and the women's faces
are dirty and lined with wisdom, with effort.

By mid-afternoon, the crowd threatens triple digits
which means the bar's closed for the first time in a decade.

"I think we need a new windmill," says a woman
with the beginning of a black eye, and another that is just
finishing.

"The saloon needs a new pianer," a man in the back says loudly.
He says it just like that, like *pianer.*

The mayor holds his hands up, quieting the crowd,
I can tell by the bulging timepiece in his breast pocket,

there will be no new *pianer*. He has some bad news friends.
Bandits came in the night, they came and, uh... they stole it away.

We had better not track them down,
because they most likely have guns, and their guns are very large.

The women's faces turn to smashed church pews,
and the men's hands wring together like worried staircases.

Test Drive

We've been test-driving this car for five days.
The police are looking for us
and we listen to their progress on the radio.

This town needs us, though;
it hasn't seen action like this since
Doc Johnson's son fell in the old well.

He'd end up with a full scholarship to NYU,
where he'd lose his virginity
and his fear of dark tunnels.

We drive fast, hugging the turns, switching lanes, changing gears,
the car and our bodies come together
like a beautiful, stolen speed machine.

We pick up hitchhikers named Carter and Stephanie.
Carter says he's a freelance brain surgeon,
and Stephanie's his first patient.

She doesn't say much but keeps insisting
she smells a freshly opened package of tropical skittles,
and we keep politely looking under the seats.

It would be three more days before they'd finally catch us,
stopped at a roadside ice cream stand,
trying to decide between Moon Mist and Rocky Road.

The car dealership owner is there, furious.
The officer leads us past him.
"You know, she handles well, but I think we'll keep looking."

These Cardboard Teeth (Summer, 1979)

We clean our teeth with the rough edges
of the cardboard we found in the lake house,

your sister, all the while, yelling at us from up on the hill.
The phone is for you.

The phone sits on a small table beside the couch,
splitting rent with a reading lamp and a hand-knit doily.

The receiver was large, black, and heavy;
it holds the voice of your great aunt Millie.

Everybody's got a great aunt Millie
if they go back far enough.

"What news of your father's health?" she demands;
you can hear that even the watered-whiskey can't fix her lisp.

"The same," you say, your voice muffled
for the cardboard still wedged between your teeth.

Out the front window, I see the neighbor's dog
walking down one side of the wheel-worn driveway.

You hang up the phone with a defeated sigh;
the receiver lands with a plastic thud that could define a generation.

Days like these seem to go on forever
but are gone before we ever know what they really are.

Triple Word Score

"When you vacuum the bedroom, I feel like we're staying in a hotel."
You say this very quietly, as if our bed is the dark door to a haunted
house.

The sugar candy in your mouth swirls around,
and clicks against the back of your teeth like a drunken metronome.

"When I vacuum the bedroom, I feel like I'm reversing a stereotype."
I reply, with a deadpan sense of accomplishment.

We sleep then, and you dream silent dreams concerning
shirtless, dark-haired, car mechanics named Ricardo.

In the bed next to you I dream of losing scrabble matches
to a polar bear in the park, two games to one.

Things get violent when I refuse to pay up,
and he tells me my face is about to get a triple word score.

In our room, dressers and the bedposts stand guard all around us,
their eyes peeled for the intruding streaks of new morning light.

The lingering silence wears a fading black coat,
and hangs around a little while longer before making an alarming exit.

I stir awake and stare out the window which frames a solid blue sky.
The crisp September morning breathes deeply, then makes itself at
home.

Banks, Pockets, and Sock Drawers

Late for work
and drunk again,
The summer sun beating down
on his sweating forehead.
He thinks of all the places people
keep their money.

His briefcase –
packed for a long stay.
Ham sandwich and a six-shooter.
He wonders if people
who aren't cowboys
even call them that anymore.

The grey carpeted half-walls
shake hands
with the blue carpeted
full-floors.
His office:
remarkably unremarkable.

He wonders what
a bullet would look like
traveling through the
water cooler.
A silver-haired swimmer,
diving from the highest board.

The police report would read
as follows:
Warning shots fired into water cooler,
takes own life.
An avid fan
of ham sandwiches.

Three Days From Now

Jacob was stealing malt liquor
when he found out his dad had cancer.
His sister from Alberta called,
and blurted it through tears before hanging up.

A liquor bottle dropped from waist height
will break exactly 74% of the time.
The beer ran under the convenience store shelving
emerging in the next aisle.

Muhammad ran the convenience store full time,
and got robbed at gunpoint part-time, on the side.

He unboxed penny candy and telephone minute cards,
and thought about the rent,
and about his old job back home, as a brain surgeon.

He wondered how many of these cards would get stolen.
(Exactly 18%)

Julie ran out of minutes on her phone mid-proposal,
devastating both parties involved.
He thought she'd hung up on him.

She swore loudly, and threw her phone at the sidewalk
(69% chance of breaking)
the phone exploded,
sending pieces of personal information in every direction.

She collapsed on the sidewalk, sobbing.
She might have even said yes.

Glen was a street sweeper with a winning lottery ticket
that wouldn't be drawn for three more days.

His father named him Glen
so that we would have the perfect name for street sweeping,
and when applying for the job,
he had added under skills & assets "My name is Glen."
He wasn't married, and had never kissed a girl,
though he thought the one crying on the sidewalk was awfully pretty.
(6% chance of a first date, 77% chance three days from now.)

Beginnings or Ends

Suddenly, as quickly as it began, it stopped.
You wake on the beach,
your ear an open tunnel for the lapping ocean waves
to press against your brain.

The engine deep inside you starts, skips, stops, and starts again.
The fans whir, and everything comes slowly to life.
The world as you've always known it
stops spinning, and turning,
and focuses in front of your glassy half-open eyes.

The sky is such a perfect flat blue
you can't decide where the sky stops
and the ocean begins.
Your skin matches the beach,
and you can't figure that out either,
what's skin or sand?
So it goes on like that for a while.
Struggling and stumbling,
uncertain about beginnings or ends.

Around you, you see the remains of a small boat, or a raft,
whatever it is that got you here in the first place.
Off the shore you can see a very large boat, anchored,
lazily cresting the waves.
You can also see a smaller boat
with people waving, and working, and coming toward you.

You think perhaps you've died and gone to a place
where you just see boats of various sizes forever and ever.

You think this a rather meek hell.
You'd have done more selfish things had you known.
Then you're struck by the notion, not of death
but of quite the opposite:

they're coming to rescue you.

You lay back down on the sand,
slipping in and out of consciousness.

The small boat is larger now.
(We're talking perspective here).
The crew is climbing out.
You want to tell them to be careful,
that the ocean will lap their brains
and fill their heads
and they will fall over, top heavy, and sink.

They seem concerned only for you
as they move and hustle.
Things are darkening again
as your head crashes back down into the soft sand.

Strong arms lift you into a boat,
and the wooden floorboards are surprisingly welcome.
Dry, despite the surrounding ocean.
The water can't hurt you here.
Your rescuers speak French and talk amongst themselves
about, what you can only assume is,
Paris, or baguettes or about wearing berets.

You imagine they're saying very important things.
You imagine they're naming delicious food.
Warm places.

The sky is the sea, your ear is a tunnel, your brain is alive.

THREE / Love, or Something Like It.

On Dentistry and Windmills

I pick you up from the dentist in Halifax
in a rental car with the roof down..

What a rush, to do something so familiar
in an unfamiliar way.

Your mouth and face went twelve rounds
with a dentist who buys watches on the internet.
"Things went well," the dentist tells me.
"Tough one though, roots were twisted."

I laugh at the drugged, alarmed look on your face
as we cross the border into New Brunswick.
The sleepy giants towering above us,
swinging their lazy arms in the fog,
waving us home like third-base coaches
with other things on their minds.

We sit on a curb in Sackville.
I eat a burger and you drink a milkshake.
You work up the mental clarity to tell me a joke,
your voice, heavy with milkshake,
with dentist's medicine.

The joke is this:
"What do you call a race with no finish line?"

Thunder cracks overhead,
and a sun-shower almost instantly darkens the sidewalk.

We put the roof up on the car,
the weight of the unfinished joke
heavy around our necks.

You sleep the rest of the way home,

and later your mother calls.
"Went well," I'm telling her.
"Tough one though, roots were twisted."

We both nod into our phones,
pretending to know exactly what that means.

Blind Date

"You don't look good when you ride a bicycle," she says.
"Your arms are too long for your torso," I reply.

Things aren't going well.

We eat sushi on a waterfront patio
and make small talk about the waves
how they never stop, never take a break.

More poetry about the ocean.

"You would look better without your glasses," she says
"Your lips can't decide who's on top," I reply

I take my glasses off.

Later, on her front step, it's dark
and things are blurry.

We stand less than an arm's length apart,
having grown on each other.

"There's a moth on your house," I say
"That's an antique doorbell," she replies

She slides my glasses back on my face.

Overhead the moon tries and fails
to contain its light.

More poetry about the moon.

The Downside of Marrying a Photographer

It doesn't make you any more handsome.

In fact, if the image was blurry and terrible,
it would be a welcome relief.

But it isn't. It's quite good – great even.
It captures the weird shape of your head
and the way that even nice clothing
require a nice place to hang them.

It captures the way you've put on some pounds
since your skateboard friends used to call you "lanky";
now your weight has caught your height and you're just "regular".

"It's quite good," I say,
my mouth doing a strange, smile-frown slow dance.

I keep staring at the photo,
trying to see the things in me she does.

Blue Monday

Our tattoos bring the rain down,
exploding on sidewalks and chain link fences
like the footsteps of an escaping shoplifter.

We rush the pawn shops and second hand stores
for nicotine-stained Super Nintendos
and worn Bradbury paperbacks.

We used to say if moonlight had a postal code
we'd write letters about sleeping on the train tracks
and waiting for your mom to come home.

These cobblestone streets bring the rain down,
exploding on tourists and their maps
that will never be folded the same way again.

We moved here last year and have gotten lost every day.
We do this on purpose because it ensures us
an ever-changing view of a lonely and beautiful city.

We lay in your bedroom, on the hardwood floor
while the cool night air saunters in through the open window,
bringing the neighbors voices in with it.

They're standing on their back deck, smoking weed
and arguing the significance of the '81 Expos.
And we laugh, and our laughter brings the rain down.

Love in a Pandemic (Day Drinking)

I'm standing in the kitchen, drunk,
eating packs of banana bread Bear Paws.

You enter, stage left, disgusted.
"What the fuck are you doing?" your face-mouth is saying.

"Whassa matter?" I say, spitting brown crumbs
"Are we saving these for the kid's *SCHOOL LUNCHES*!?"

"Get a hold of yourself," you're saying.
God, you're beautiful when you're mad at me about eating bear paws.

Later, in the upstairs place of the house,
I lay exactly face-down on the floor beside the bed.

I want to know what it feels like to BE a bed.

I can hear your impatient sigh from above.
"You know, just because there's a pandemic going on
doesn't give you free reign to act like a complete idiot"

I don't reply, and we lay like that, in the quiet room.

The window is open slightly,
letting the evening's birdsong fill the space where the talking used to.

Swift, Violent, Quiet, Beautiful

I caught you treating autumn
like a swift, and violent end.

As if summer
was the only time
memories could be made.

As if the declining afternoon highs
were a hurdle
to learning how to love.

A credence unearned,
as surely the reddening leaves
whisper promises
of a quiet,
and beautiful future.

Things Unsaid

I'm picking her up from work.

Her breath plumes
as she climbs in the February car.

"Today felt like 2 days,"
she says, desperately.

I say nothing.

"We need milk,
and the girls need snow pants,
and my job sucks,
and my back hurts,"
she continues.

What she actually means to say is,
"I love you."

I still say nothing,

but it's a pregnant nothing -
an uncomfortable one.

A silence I've learned to fill with nonsense.

"You know," I start,
"I saw a girl holding a rabbit the other day
and I got to thinking.
In my whole life
I think I've probably held more than 5...
but definitely less than 10 rabbits."

She's quiet this time.

And what I actually mean to say is,
"I love you, too."

Catastrophic Failure

You're on another planet
when you collide with the coffee table.

Chasing dragons, or riding unicorns,
dodging ninjas, in the nick of time.

You fail to dodge the sharp corner
of the Ikea centerpiece, however.

The connection made into your soft ribs:
a catastrophic failure.

Your wail; a siren song,
filling the house with an urgency.

I'm first on the scene,
scooping you in my arms.

I scoop greedily in these years,
while the scooping's still good.

I take the weight of you,
feeling your quickened heartbeat.

Your cry is sharp in my ear
but quiets as you slump, heavy on my chest.

These are the days easily fixed.
A hold, and a hushed tone,

small plastic bowls
of mac and cheese.

Early Morning, Somewhere

When the end is finally upon us,
we head to the beach to watch it unfold.

We write swears on the edge of the ocean
while the sun rises against our backs.

What hearts are these that could love the beach's
most vulnerable, toe-stubbing thoughts,
printed on its yawning forehead?

What hands are these?
Laced around coffee mugs of wine,
our lips and teeth, purple with the effort.

Only the dog knows the truth of it,
and only for an instant:
white-washed legs and a tongue of sand.

Later, our bodies will ache with acquired wisdom.
The ocean will erase the foul language,
our mugs will sit empty,
and the world never ends.

On Storms and Soup

You're the type of person
who has a strong opinion on soups.
That's opinion, not onion.
Which is not to say
you don't have a strong opinion
of onion soup.

You embrace late-season,
early-April snowstorms,
saying they are there
to keep our Canadian entitlement in check.
I say nothing,
slipping my boots on
and silently refusing to clear the driveway.

We go back and forth like that,
half-hearted opinions,
on things that don't matter.

Me, clearing the snow off your car,
and you,
making soup.

I'm not sure, ask Dad

I feel like
at any given time
I am only 60% of the way to understanding
how ice cream is made.

Our footsteps on the wooded path
bark beneath us
As the muffled bones
of one thousand fallen leaves
cry out a failing snap.

"Dad?"
Comes the prompt.

"Yes, dear?"
The reply.

"Which part of the cow
does the ice cream *cone* come from?"

Maybe I know less than I think I do.

Certainly less
than she thinks I do.

"The cone comes from the cow's teeth, dear."

Her contemplative silence is acceptance,
and I feel guilty almost immediately.

Our footsteps murder more leaves.

I guess I feel guilty about that too.

2:45 AM

There's nothing that exists at 2:45 AM
you can't see from the edge of a mall's roof.

We scour the city, looking for love.
We climb trees and hang from playground structures.

We ask everyone we meet if they've seen it.
We open dumpsters and yell into the stinking abyss:

"Are you love? Are you in there?" And it whispers back:
"No. We are not love. We are baby raccoons instead."

At home, later, the warmth rubs our red cheeks
as we sit cross-legged by the light of the Christmas tree.

In the fridge: a half bottle of dark beer.
We drink from small cups, and it warms us from the inside.

Sweet Ruin

She used to turn the blinker on 30 seconds out,
coasting to the intersection –
"I like to slowly become more relevant,
like fusion restaurants, or a stopped clock."

"Do you want to know something else about me?" She asked,
and I almost laughed because,
despite the fact that she was a terrible driver,
I wanted to know everything about her.

So we talked like that for the rest of the day.
A real question-and-answer, forget-the-time talk.
When it started getting dark, we found light;
When it started getting light, we found coffee.

Sitting in the red booths across from each other,
we could see forever unfolding before our eyes.
"Do you know why I drink my coffee black?" she asked.
"Because you want it to match your soul?" I joked.

She laughed, and we built tiny houses on the table using sugar
packets,
and I imagined living in a home like that.
Each rainy day slowly eating away at the walls and floors,
real life slowly creeping in through the sweet ruin.

The Very Worst Time to Talk About Pencils

She has a mouth full of cereal
and her hair up with a pencil.

The pencil has a lot of eraser left,
and I want to tell her that the pencil

would be a very good pencil
to use as a pencil, and not as a hair thing.

This strikes me as a strictly asshole thing to say,
but it's just that we have better pencils for such things,

ones with little to no eraser,
or crummy leads that are always broken.

Pencils made in crappy factories
or by failing companies that don't always make pencils so well.

She asks what we're going to do today,
and I can't concentrate, and I want to tell her

that we should probably buy some hair clips
or at the very least some knock-off pencils.

But now I've taken too long to answer
and she's giving me a look

that says this is probably the very worst time
to talk about pencils.

The Long Way to Alone

I

Outside, the moon is close enough to touch,
but we're mostly concerning ourselves with the wine table.

Your sister's boyfriend is telling stories
about his mission trip to a country with a "Z" in the name.

He nods, and tucks his hair a lot,
and I'm struggling to think of a question that makes me sound
interested.

I'm listening to an argument taking place near the TV
when someone offers me a small plastic cup:

"Here, drink this. It will make you feel like a security guard
who is constantly searching for a better parking spot."

II

You're filing taxes with your hair up;
I could write an entire novel about a photograph of you.

We're both considering our impending dental appointments,
and I'm working on what to wear —and when to start flossing.

We're laying on the thinly carpeted second floor
of a townhouse your parents are renting, and you were sick, even then.

I am uneasy with the lack of commitment implied
by renting, by townhouses, and by being sick.

Later, we watch a movie with a talking mouse in it.
The mouse isn't really talking, but they make him look like he is.

III

It's summer now, so we're showing arms and legs
as if they're a secret the snow can't find out about.

I pass a man buying plastic plumbing at the hardware store,
carefully measuring and fitting pieces together: a puzzle for water.

He's talking to himself in half-inches and one-eighths,
his hands —the color of my car's wheel-wells.

Later, I find an old movie ticket in a thin jacket.
The movie starred a man with a face like a diamond.

We crowded in the dark theatre to watch his jawline move
and watch the silhouettes eat popcorn.

IV

The sun is setting again, a friendly reminder it has other places to be.
We're inside whispering super obvious truths about bridges.

"They get you across water, and you don't get wet," you say.
"They're not on the ground, but the ends of them are," I reply.

No one needs us or cares where we are, so we're here,
laying on the couch, our legs entwined: a puzzle for people.

A news anchor with hair like an apology
explains why the world is basically terrible.

Before bed we use a pen to write on our hands and arms,
reminders for morning: "You're beautiful. The sun will be back."

V

Hospital time is real time doubled
then divided by the waistline of the nurse with whom you have
the best chance.

The man sitting across from me had been tying his shoe for
twenty minutes,
and I can see the dying wife all over his face and wonder if he sees
the same on mine.

Behind me, a woman with a voice like a deep fryer
tells an insensitive joke about the afterlife.

I've gotten too old for confrontations like that,
so I stare at my hands and imagine the lines are the adventures
we've mapped out.

When they call your name, it skids across the waxed floor tiles
and hits the windows overlooking the moon-lit parking lot.

VI

Watching your sickness feels like opening an umbrella in the
kitchen.
The lawn needs mowing; the mailbox is full of second notices.

We watch Ghostbusters and laugh when Bill gets slimed.
The ghosts aren't real, but they make them look like they are.

Your face is the next great American novel.
I'm not writing it, but I'm reading it every single day.

Your arms are the shape of table legs,
and I believe there was a time when your arms didn't worry me.

The neighbors make me a casserole, and I chew slowly to keep it
down.

The night air hums with a loss so large and a moon, close enough to touch.

Acknowledgements

Some of these poems appeared as earlier versions in print and online zines, such as *Snap! Magazine, Red Fez, Volume, The Tempest, Hard Times in the Maritimes and It's Burning Off*. To these publications, thank you for taking the time to consider and publish my work.

I want to thank Jordan Trethewey, Ryan Griffith, and Leo Lafleur for the honest feedback and for the help refining this collection. Thanks to Mike Romard and Corenski Nowlan for listening to and commenting on some of these writings all those years ago (Vagabond Trust, never say die!)

Thanks to Rachel Bryant for her editing skills and for teaching me I have literally no idea how a comma is used. Thanks to Pamela Pierce for the amazing artwork, and patience to perfectly realize my vision.

Thanks to the crew at The Write Cup bookstore in Saint John. Your space is more important than you even know.

Special thanks to Amy for a tireless, endless supply of encouragement, patience, and feedback. Thank you for arguing with me to make things better. Thanks for the photo and making me look good. Thanks for the love. Thanks to Lena and Harper for being my chaotic muses.

Thank you for reading.

Support your local art scene.

Jordan's works have been published in various journals both in the print and digital media all across North America. This is his third book of poetry and fourth published work of writing. Jordan lives in Grand Bay-Westfield, New Brunswick, with his beautiful wife and two energetic daughters.

www.ingramcontent.com/pod-product-compliance
Lightning Source LLC
Chambersburg PA
CBHW020803130626
46554CB00006B/2297